200 Meditations for 200 Beads

Ten Meditations for each
of the 20 Mysteries of the Rosary

Robert Theophilus

LEONINE PUBLISHERS
PHOENIX, ARIZONA

Published by

Leonine Publishers LLC
Phoenix, Arizona, USA

ISBN-13: 978-1-942190-72-1

Library of Congress Control Number: 2024924377

Printed in the United States of America

10 9 8 7 6 5 4 3 2 1

Visit us online at www.leoninepublishers.com
For more information: info@leoninepublishers.com

Contents

Part I

Part II

Part I

❧

Introduction

[A] *Hail or Rejoice?*

What follows within this section "Hail or Rejoice?" is derived from *Jesus of Nazareth: The Infancy Narratives* by Pope Benedict XVI and from *Rethinking Mary in the New Testament* by Edward Sri.

At the Annunciation, the Angel Gabriel does not address Mary with the usual Hebrew greeting *shalom*. Instead, Gabriel's greeting to Mary is literally a command: *chaire*, "rejoice." In the Old Testament, this exact same command is used by both the prophet Zephaniah 3:14 and the prophet Zechariah 9:9 to call daughter Zion to share in the future joy when God will come as king. Zephaniah also tells daughter Zion that the Lord is in her midst and that she should fear evil no more, so Gabriel tells Mary that the Lord is with her and do not be afraid. Just as God is about to come to dwell within the walls of Zion, so too the Lord is about to dwell within the womb of Mary. Zechariah uses the command *chaire* to invite God's people to rejoice over the king coming to Jerusalem. He will bring peace to the nations. Similarly, Gabriel tells Mary to rejoice for the King of Israel is coming to her. He describes her child as the One who will be given the throne of his father David and whose kingdom will have no end.

For hundreds of years the Jews longed for these prophecies to be fulfilled. Now, at the Annunciation to Mary, the long anticipated moment has finally arrived. All of this tells us that the prayer to Our Lady should not begin with Hail Mary full of grace but with Rejoice full of grace. (Rejoice, for I bring you good news; rejoice, for the Lord is with you; rejoice, for you are daughter Zion in person.)

[B] *Rosarium Virginis Mariae*

In 2002, Pope Saint John Paul II published an Apostolic Letter entitled **Rosarium Virginis Mariae (RVM)** to instruct the faithful on the proper way to both understand and pray the rosary. Unfortunately, many Catholics are not aware of the contents of this letter and, consequently, pray the rosary in a manner that is directly opposite to what the pope recommended. Moreover, and again contrary to the pope's counsel, they make the rosary an end in itself, rather than a means to an end. The purpose of this introductory section is to familiarize readers with *Rosarium Virginis Mariae*. John Paul II often quotes Pope Saint Paul VI, so it is to be stressed, therefore, that what follows are the words of two canonized popes (with my own comments added parenthetically).

[C] *Praying the Rosary*

(a) *The Crucifix*

The first thing to note is that the rosary begins with a Crucifix. This tells us that the rosary is focused on Christ and His mysteries. The beads loop away from and then return to the Crucifix, indicating that Jesus is the alpha and the omega, the beginning and the end of our prayer and of our life.

(b) *Our Lady and the Rosary*

Mary has a mother's care for the pilgrim Church. The rosary transports us to Mary's side where she sets before us the mysteries of her Son. We ask Mary to help us see and venerate each mystery through her eyes and to love them through her heart. In imitation of Mary we also keep all these things and ponder them in our hearts.

(c) *The Mechanics of Praying the Rosary*

The rosary is a typically meditative prayer (*RVM* 5). "Without this contemplative dimension, it would lose its meaning, as Pope Paul VI clearly pointed out: 'Without contemplation, the Rosary is a body without a soul' [underline added] (that is, lifeless and dead), 'and its recitation runs the risk of becoming a mechanical repetition of formulas, in violation of the admonition of Christ'" (in other words, the near occasion of sin) (*RVM* 12).

"In effect, the Rosary is simply *a method of contemplation*. As a method, it serves as a means to an end and cannot become an end in itself" [underline added] (*RVM* 28). (In other words, don't just "say it" to fulfill some sort of mandate.)

> Otherwise there is a risk that the Rosary would not only fail to produce the intended spiritual effects, but even that the beads, with which it is usually said, could come to be regarded as

some kind of amulet or magic object, thereby radically distorting their meaning and function (*RVM* 28).

At present, in different parts of the Church, there are many ways to introduce the Rosary. In some places, it is customary to begin with the opening words of Psalm 70: "O God, come to my aid; O Lord, make haste to help me," as if to nourish in those who are praying a humble awareness of their own insufficiency.... The Rosary is then ended with a prayer for the intentions of the Pope, as if to expand the vision of the one praying to embrace all the needs of the Church. It is precisely in order to encourage this ecclesial dimension of the Rosary that the Church has seen fit to grant indulgences to those who recite it with the required dispositions (*RVM* 37).

(d) *Focusing on the Name Jesus*

Pope John Paul II states in *RVM* that the center of gravity in the rejoice full of grace prayer,

the hinge as it were which joins its two parts, is *the name of Jesus*. Sometimes, in hurried recitation, this centre of gravity can be overlooked, and with it the connection to the mystery of Christ being contemplated. Yet it is precisely the emphasis given to the name of **Jesus** and to his mystery that is the <u>sign of a meaningful</u>

and fruitful recitation of the Rosary [under-
line added]. Pope Paul VI drew attention, in
his Apostolic Exhortation *Marialis Cultus*, to
the custom in certain regions of highlighting
the name of Christ by the addition of a clause
referring to the mystery being contemplated
(RVM 33).

For example, when contemplating the first glorious
mystery, one could say on one of the beads: Rejoice full of
grace, the Lord is with you, blessed are you among wom-
en and blessed is the fruit of your womb **Jesus** [emphasis
added]—Why do you look for the Living One amongst
the dead?—holy Mary, Mother of God, pray for us sinners,
etc., and on the next bead: Rejoice full of grace, the Lord
is with you, blessed are you among women and blessed is
the fruit of your womb **Jesus** [emphasis added]—whose
love was as strong as death—holy Mary, Mother of God,
pray for us sinners, etc. (See also *The Threefold Garland*
by Hans von Balthasar.)

This is a praiseworthy custom…. It gives force-
ful expression to our faith in Christ, directed
to the different moments of the Redeemer's
life. It is at once *a profession of faith* and an aid
in concentrating our meditation…. When we
repeat the name of Jesus – the only name giv-
en to us by which we may hope for salvation
(cf. Acts 4:12) – in close association with the
name of his Blessed Mother, almost as if it were
done at her suggestion, we set out on a path of

assimilation meant to help us enter more deeply into the life of Christ (*RVM* 33).

To "remember" Christ's life, death and resurrection "in a spirit of faith and love <u>is to be open to the grace which Christ won for us" by these mysteries</u>" [underline added] (*RVM* 13).

(e) *The "Our Father"*

After focusing on the mystery,

> it is natural for the mind to be lifted up towards the Father. In each of his mysteries, <u>Jesus always leads us to the Father</u>, for as he rests in the Father's bosom (cf. Jn 1:18) he is continually turned towards him. He wants us to share in his intimacy with the Father, so that we can say with him: "Abba, Father" (Rom 8:15; Gal 4:6) (*RVM* 32).

We must listen in the Spirit to the Father's voice inasmuch as "no one knows the Son except the Father (Mt 11:27)" (*RVM* 18).

(f) *Trinitarian Doxology*

> It is important that the *Gloria, the high-point of Christian contemplation*, be given due prominence in the Rosary. In public recitation it could be sung, as a way of giving proper emphasis to the essentially Trinitarian structure of all Christian prayer (*RVM* 34).

Part II

ℰↄ

200 Meditations for 200 Beads

The following is a set of meditations that one can use after stopping at the name **Jesus** in the center of the prayers to Our Lady that, collectively, make up the framework of the rosary.

The Joyful Mysteries

ℭℌ

First Joyful Mystery

The Angel Gabriel Announces the Coming of the Long-Awaited Messiah

First Bead: The Angel Gabriel was sent from God, to a virgin, and the virgin's name was Mary (Lk 1:26-27). The angel was sent by God; this is God's initiative. Salvation is a gift, but mankind must cooperate with grace.

Second Bead: And the angel said to her: "Rejoice full of grace! The Lord is with you" (Lk 1:28). Rejoice, for I bring you good news. Rejoice, for you have found favor with God.

Third bead: Gabriel asks Mary whether she will consent to be the mother of the Messiah. He goes on to say that her child "will be called Son of the Most High, and of His kingdom there will be no end" (Lk 1:32-33). Mary is being asked to become the mother of the Son of God; it is a wonder that she remains calm.

Fourth Bead: Mary inquires of Gabriel how she can obey his request while remaining a consecrated virgin (Lk 1:34). Mary is not doubting the angel; she is simply asking for clarification.

Fifth Bead: Gabriel replies: "The Holy Spirit will come upon you and the power of the Most High will overshadow you. Therefore the child to be born will be called holy, the Son of God" (Lk 1:35). The angel tells Mary that God, Himself, will be the child's Father, so she will conceive miraculously as a virgin.

Sixth Bead: Mary gives her consent: "Behold I am the handmaid of the Lord. May it be done to me according to your word" (Lk 1:38). In spite of all that her yes implies, Mary expresses a joyous desire to be at the Lord's service, as she longs to be His lowly handmaid. Her response is exemplary for all ages.

Seventh Bead: Mary is the archetype of the Church, the bride of Christ. Consequently, her response is spousal, like the deliberately uttered "I will" of a bride to her groom.

Eighth Bead: Mary's response is absolute; no hint of a hesitation or objection. She doesn't attempt to negotiate or find a way out. Her answer is simply "Let it be!" And the Word became flesh.

Ninth Bead: Gabriel informs Mary that her elderly kins-woman Elizabeth is now six months pregnant with John the Baptist. Owing to her advanced age, Elizabeth has also conceived miraculously, although by natural means.

Tenth Bead: We end the first mystery with some of the most inspiring words in scripture: "For nothing shall be impossible to God" (Lk 1:37). It reminds us of the angel's words to Abraham and Sarah: "Why did Sarah laugh? Is anything too marvelous for the Lord to do?" (Gen 18:14).

Personal Notes:

Second Joyful Mystery

Mary Visits Her Kinswoman Elizabeth

First Bead: Realizing that Elizabeth will need help, Mary goes to assist her during her final months of pregnancy. Mary is the first missionary, the first to bring the good news. This visitation is also Mary's first charitable act as Mother of the Church.

Second Bead: Upon hearing Mary's greeting, Elizabeth is filled with the Holy Spirit and cries out with a loud voice (Lk 1:41-42). God is speaking through Elizabeth.

Third Bead: Elizabeth praises Mary: "Blessed is the fruit of your womb" (Lk 1:42). Luke is pointing out that Mary is the new Eve. The original Eve listened to the bad angel (Satan) and accepted the bad (forbidden) fruit; Mary, the new Eve, listened to the good angel (Gabriel) and accepted the good fruit (Jesus) into her womb (Brian Mullady OP: *"Captivated by the Master"*).

Fourth Bead: Elizabeth is humble. "And how does it happen to me that the mother of my Lord should come to me?" (Lk 1:43). Here Elizabeth refers to Mary as the Theotokos, the God-bearer or Mother of God.

Fifth Bead: Elizabeth continues: "At the moment the sound of your greeting reached my ears, the infant in my womb leaped for joy" (Lk 1:44). The Messianic child blesses John the Baptist while he is still in his mother. Baby John also leaps to admonish his mother from within (*Hans von Balthasar: "The Threefold Garland"*).

Sixth Bead: Elizabeth refers to Mary as the archetypal believer and woman of faith: "Blessed are you who believed that what was spoken to you by the Lord would be fulfilled" (Lk 1:45).

Seventh Bead: Mary is also humble; in her Magnificat she redirects all this praise toward God. Although she is without sin, Mary is also one of the redeemed: "My spirit rejoices in God my savior" (Lk 1:47). This speaks of her Immaculate Conception.

Eighth Bead: Mary continues: "From this day forward all generations will call me blessed" (Lk 1:48). Elizabeth is the first to do so when she proclaims: "Blessed are you among women." Those who pray the rosary also fulfill this prophesy.

Ninth Bead: Mary's first Christian occupation consisted of keeping house for Elizabeth. Often, our Christian life means doing small things with great love.

Tenth Bead: Here we see two country women rejoicing together over the great things God has done for them.

Personal Notes:

Third Joyful Mystery

The Birth of Jesus in Bethlehem

First Bead: During the reign of Caesar Augustus, when Quirinius was governor of Syria, all were ordered to return to their own town for a census. The birth of Jesus is not a myth; it occurred at a precisely defined time and place.

Second Bead: When Joseph and Mary arrive in Bethlehem, there is no room for them in the inn. Perhaps this is because they come from Galilee of the Gentiles. Even before He is born, Jesus suffers rejection. Make room for the Holy Family in your heart and for Jesus in your life.

Third Bead: Joseph and Mary take refuge in a cave that is being used as a stable. Here Mary brings forth her firstborn Son. Saint Paul goes on to say that Jesus is the first born of many brethren (Rom 8:29). Humanity begins anew with Jesus.

Fourth Bead: The poverty surrounding the "newborn king" is palpable. Animals, humans, and angels, all three orders of creation, are there to worship the Christ Child. Mary lays Jesus in a feeding trough, indicating that He is the Bread of Life.

Fifth Bead: Imagine how Mary's heart glowed with the tender love of a mother for her baby and the profound adoration of a soul before her God.

Sixth Bead: Because God acts outside of time, within the eternal now, we also can come to the manger to worship the newborn King.

Seventh Bead: The angels appear to poor shepherds in their fields; they are the first to hear the good news: "Today a savior has been born for you" (Lk 2:11). The shepherds go to Bethlehem and tell Joseph and Mary all that they heard from the angel.

Eighth Bead: "And Mary kept all these things, reflecting on them in her heart" (Lk 2:19). In the person of Mary, the Church already pondered the meaning of Christmas. We also must meditate upon the significance of Christmas within our own hearts.

Ninth Bead: Wise men also come from the east; gentiles seeking the Jewish Messiah. They find the new king with Mary, His Queen Mother, and they bring Him gifts of gold (Jesus is king), incense (Jesus is priest), and myrrh (Jesus is savior) (Mt 2:11).

Tenth Bead: The wise men are also known as kings. The shepherds find their Shepherd and the kings find their King.

Personal Notes:

Fourth Joyful Mystery

Jesus is Presented in the Temple

First Bead: Joseph and Mary bring Jesus to the Temple. For Mary's "purification" they offer two pigeons as they are too poor to provide a lamb. They have, however, brought the true "Lamb of God."

Second Bead: The parents of a first-born child must offer him to God. Subsequently, they can receive the child back by providing a compensatory gift. There is no mention, however, of redeeming Jesus. It would appear that He is handed over to God once and for all.

Third Bead: There is a devout man named Simeon in the Temple and God has revealed to him that he will not die until he has seen the Lord's Messiah.

Fourth Bead: Simeon takes Jesus and blesses God, saying: "Now, Master, you may dismiss your servant in peace, according to your word, for my eyes have seen your salvation, which you prepared in the sight of all the peoples, a light for revelation to the Gentiles, and glory for your people Israel" (Lk 2:29-32).

Fifth Bead: Simeon calls Jesus a light for revelation to the Gentiles. In doing so he implies that Jesus is the suffering servant of Isaiah in whom Galilee, that impure land of darkness, will see a great light (Isaiah 9:2).

Sixth Bead: Simeon also refers to Jesus as "glory for your people Israel." When the Ark of the Covenant was taken from the Temple, God's glory no longer dwelt there. Now as Mary, the new Ark of the Covenant, brings Jesus to the Temple, God's glory returns.

Seventh Bead: Simeon goes on to prophesy that Jesus will be a sign that will be contradicted and that a sword will also pierce Mary's soul (Lk 2:34-35). Jesus will endure opposition to His mission all the way to the contradiction of the Cross.

Eighth Bead: The Church, the Body of Christ, will also be a sign of contradiction through the centuries, and Mary, the Ecclesia Immaculata, will have to share in this suffering.

Ninth Bead: We should imitate Simeon's faith and patience, for even though he was already old, God eventually kept His promise to him and he saw the Lord's anointed.

<u>**Tenth Bead:**</u> There was a prophetess named Anna who also spoke about the child Jesus to all who were awaiting the redemption of Jerusalem. Simeon and Anna represent faithful Israel, and are there to greet the Messiah when He comes to the Temple.

Personal Notes:

Fifth Joyful Mystery

Jesus Is Lost and Then Found in the Temple

First Bead: Mary and Joseph take the 12-year-old Jesus to Jerusalem for Passover. On the way back, Mary and Joseph assume that Jesus is with relatives in the caravan, but after a day and a half they realize that He is missing.

Second Bead: They return to Jerusalem and after searching for three days they find Jesus in the Temple. He is talking with the elders, and all who heard Him were astounded at His understanding and His answers (Lk 2:47). Something greater than Solomon is here.

Third Bead: Mary asks Jesus: "Son, why have you done this to us? Your father and I have been looking for you with great anxiety" (Lk 2:48). Jesus replied: "Why were you looking for me? Did you not know that I must be in my Father's house?" (Lk 2:49).

Fourth Bead: The 12-year-old Jesus begins to indicate that He knows who He is and what His mission is. He proclaims the radical nature of the Gospel in which even the closest of human relationships are challenged by the demands of the Kingdom.

Fifth Bead: Jesus asks: "Why were you looking for me, did you not know that you would find me in the mystery of the three days, of my being lost and found again, of my dying and my rising that you celebrate on your altar?"

Sixth Bead: Later, during His public ministry, Mary would lose Him for three years instead of three days. Even under these circumstances, however, she continued to trust and remained faithful.

Seventh Bead: "He went down with them and was obedient to them. And Jesus advanced in wisdom and age and favor before God and man" (Lk 2:51-52). Saint Thomas says that Jesus advanced in experiential wisdom in His human nature, not the divine wisdom always present in His divine nature.

Eighth Bead: "And Mary kept all these things in her heart" (Lk 2:51). This is the second time Luke mentions this, suggesting that Mary often contemplated the mysteries associated with her Son's life.

Ninth Bead: How hard do we search for Jesus when we have lost Him due to our sins?

Tenth Bead: Are we willing to leave our home to go and stay in our Father's house in order to attend to our Father's business?

<u>*Personal Notes*</u>:

The Luminous Mysteries

❧

First Luminous Mystery

Jesus Accepts John's Baptism

First Bead: For almost 500 years Israel has been without a prophet. Now a new prophet has appeared. The message of John the Baptist crying out in the wilderness, "Prepare the way of the Lord," creates great expectations (Mt 3:3).

Second Bead: Jesus comes to John for baptism. John protests that he needs to be baptized by Jesus, but Jesus replies: "Allow it for now, for it is fitting that we fulfill all righteousness" (Mt 3:15). Jesus has come to stand in the place of sinners.

Third Bead: When Jesus comes up from the water, "the heavens were opened and He saw the Spirit of God descending upon Him" (Lk 3:21-22). Later Jesus would say: "The Spirit of God is upon me, because He has anointed me to bring glad tidings to the poor" (Lk 4:18).

Fourth Bead: And a voice came from heaven: "You are my beloved Son, with you I am well pleased" (Lk 3:22). Later Jesus would say "the Father Himself has testified about me" (John 5:37). Soon, thereafter, the evil one will tempt Jesus in the desert: "If you are the Son of God—" (Mt 4:3,6).

Fifth Bead: The baptism of Jesus is a Trinitarian event, with the Father who speaks from the cloud, the Son who is baptized, and the Holy Spirit who descends like a dove.

Sixth Bead: Jesus tells Nicodemus: "No one can enter the Kingdom of God without being born of water and Spirit" (Jn 3:3). Baptism and not circumcision is the new rite of initiation.

Seventh Bead: "When Peter was asked: 'What are we to do?' he replied: 'Repent and be baptized in the name of Jesus Christ for the forgiveness of your sins and you will receive the gift of the Holy Spirit'" (Acts 2:37-38).

Eighth Bead: "Are you unaware that we who were baptized into Christ Jesus were baptized into His death? We were indeed buried with Him through baptism, so that just as Christ was raised from the dead, we too might live in newness of life" (Rom 6:3-4).

Ninth Bead: "For in one Spirit we were all baptized into one body" (1 Cor 12:13). Baptism makes us members of the Body of Christ.

Tenth Bead: Both Saint Paul and Saint Peter agree that baptism is necessary for salvation. "He saved us through the bath of rebirth and renewal by the Holy Spirit" (Titus 3:5); "Baptism, which saves you now" (1 Peter 3:21).

Personal Notes:

Second Luminous Mystery

A Wedding Banquet at Cana

First Bead: Jesus, our Blessed Mother, and some of the Apostles go to a banquet at Cana in Galilee. Our Lady notices that the bridegroom is running out of wine. How attentive Mary is to other people's need.

Second Bead: Moved with compassion, and at her own initiative, Mary appeals to Jesus: "They have no wine" (Jn 2:3). It is as if she is appealing for all of mankind.

Third Bead: Jesus replies: "Woman, how does your concern affect me? My hour has not yet come" (Jn 2:4). Jesus calls Mary "Woman" to indicate that she is the new Eve, whose Son will crush the head of the serpent and fulfill Genesis 3:15.

Fourth Bead: When Jesus says to Mary: "My hour has not yet come," He is reminding her that to do what she is asking, He will have to perform His first public miracle and the march toward His hour will begin. Are you ready for that?

Fifth Bead: With complete trust in Jesus, Mary says to the servants what she says to all people of all time: "Do whatever He tells you" (Jn 2:5).

Sixth Bead: In response to Mary's request, Jesus tells the servants to fill the jars with water. In essence He is saying, "I will work my miracle but you must also do your part. Put in your ordinary (water), and I will change it into my miraculous (wine)."

Seventh Bead: Jesus turns the water into very good wine. By providing wine for the guests Jesus shows that He is the true messianic Bridegroom.

Eighth Bead: The goodness of the new wine and its abundance point ahead to what Jesus will give us in the Eucharist.

Ninth Bead: At the wedding banquet in Cana and in response to His mother, Jesus turns water into wine. Later at the request of His bride the Church, He will come and celebrate the eternal wedding banquet with us here and now.

Tenth Bead: When we are having doubts, we can turn to that good Mother, for it was at her request that Jesus worked a miracle that brought His disciples to faith.

Personal Notes:

Third Luminous Mystery

Proclamation of the Kingdom

First Bead: Jesus proclaims: "The Kingdom of God is at hand, repent and believe the good news!" (Mk 1:15). God is doing something that surpasses everything that happened previously. Mankind must respond with conversion and faith.

Second Bead: "The Kingdom of God is in your midst." Jesus, Himself, by His person, words, and works makes the Kingdom present. The Church also makes the Kingdom present.

Third Bead: "The Kingdom of God is like a mustard seed" (Mk 4:31). It is very small but once sown it becomes the largest of trees. This assures us of the eventual success of the Church.

Fourth Bead: "The Kingdom of God is like yeast that a woman took and mixed with wheat flour until the whole batch of dough was leavened" (Lk 13:21). The parable, once again, assures us of the powerful growth of the Kingdom, even from small beginnings.

Fifth Bead: The Kingdom of Heaven will be like ten bridesmaids who went out to meet the bridegroom. The foolish took their lamps but no oil, while the wise took both oil and their lamps. The wise could not share their oil with the foolish as the kind of oil that is needed (e.g., obedience) is not shareable. Be ready at all times.

Sixth Bead: "The Kingdom of Heaven is like a pearl of great piece" (Mt 13:45-46). It is worth sacrificing everything in order to possess it. Jesus, Himself, is that pearl.

Seventh Bead: The Kingdom of Heaven is like laborers in God's vineyard. Those who worked all day expected, but did not receive, a greater reward than those who worked only one hour. Eternal happiness depends on loving God simply because He is God.

Eighth Bead: The Kingdom of Heaven is like a servant who was forgiven a huge debt by his master, but refused to forgive a fellow servant a very small debt. The incredible gift of God's forgiveness is a gift we must share. "Forgive us our trespasses, as we forgive those who trespass against us."

Ninth Bead: The Kingdom of Heaven is like a king who gave a marriage feast for his son. Those who were invited refused to come, so the king summoned those from the street and the hedges. Jesus' mission to the Israelites was rejected and so He turned to sinners and the Gentiles. Not all who are called will remain chosen.

Tenth Bead: "Seek first the Kingdom of God and his righteousness, and all these things will be given you besides" (Mt 6:33). If we preoccupy ourselves with things that turn our attention away from God, our lives will be empty. Jesus makes the Kingdom present, so we are asking for union with Him.

Personal Notes:

Fourth Luminous Mystery

Jesus is Transfigured

First Bead: Jesus took Peter, James, and John and led them up a high mountain. And He was transfigured before them; His face shone like the sun (*lumen de lumine*) and His clothes became white as light. Jesus reveals His divinity to His apostles to strengthen them for what lay ahead.

Second Bead: And there appeared to Him Moses (the Law) and Elijah (the prophets) and they were conversing with Him about the exodus He was about to accomplish in Jerusalem.

Third Bead: A bright cloud cast a shadow over them, then from the cloud came a voice that said: "This is my beloved Son, with whom I am well pleased; listen to Him" (Mt 17:5).

Fourth Bead: Christ is the One to whom we must listen; it is in Him that the great multiplicity (in many and various ways) of the former revelation of God has been summed up (Hans von Balthasar: *"Prayer"*).

Fifth Bead: "Listen to Him because in giving us His Son, His only Word, He spoke everything to us at once and He has nothing more to say" (Saint John of the Cross). Jesus is the Torah in person.

Sixth Bead: Let us pray for all those who invent every excuse possible to justify not listening to Jesus.

Seventh Bead: Once again we see a Trinitarian event: the Father's voice, the Son, and the Holy Spirit manifesting Himself as a bright cloud.

Eighth Bead: In fact, we encounter all of salvation history: the Law, the Prophets, Christ and His Church.

Ninth Bead: After the cloud lifted, Jesus (who fulfills the Law and the Prophets) was found alone. He came to them and said: "Rise, and do not be afraid" (Mt 17:7).

Tenth Bead: Jesus charged them: "Do not tell the vision to anyone until the Son of Man has been raised from the dead" (Mt 17:9). And they wondered what rising from the dead meant.

Personal Notes:

Fifth Luminous Mystery

Jesus Institutes the Eucharist

First Bead: "The Eucharist is 'the source and summit of the Christian life.' ...For in the blessed Eucharist is contained the whole spiritual good of the Church, namely Christ Himself" (*Catechism of the Catholic Church*, 1324).

Second Bead: The Mass is the memorial in which our Lord's sacrifice is perpetuated throughout time. The Mass does not add to or multiply the sacrifice of the Cross; rather it renders that sacrifice sacramentally present on the altar (Pope John Paul II: *"Encyclical on the Most Holy Eucharist"* (12)).

Third Bead: The Eucharist makes present not only the mystery of the Savior's passion and death, but also the mystery of His resurrection. It is as the risen and living One that Christ can become in the Eucharist, the Bread of Life.

Fourth Bead: In the Eucharist we also receive the pledge of our own bodily resurrection at the end of the world. Christ assures us: "He who eats my flesh and drinks my blood has eternal life and I will raise him up on the last day" (Jn 6:54).

Fifth Bead: The Eucharist reinforces our communion with the Church in heaven. We become united to the heavenly Liturgy and become part of that great multitude that cries out: "Salvation belongs to our God and to the Lamb." The Mass is, therefore, an actual experiencing of heaven on earth (Pope John Paul II: *"Encyclical on the Most Holy Eucharist"* (19)).

Sixth Bead: The Eucharist also expresses and brings about the unity of the faithful who form one body in Christ. Saint Paul reminds us in 1 Corinthians 10:17: "Because there is one bread, we who are many are one body because we partake of the one loaf."

Seventh Bead: When we offer up the divine victim during the sacrifice of the Mass, we also offer up ourselves. Christ on the Cross prays not only as head of the body, but He also enfolds into His prayer all the supplications of His mystical body.

Eighth Bead: Saint Paul, therefore, urges us to scrutinize our conscience before receiving communion. "Whoever, therefore, eats the bread or drinks the cup of the Lord in an unworthy manner will be guilty of profaning the body and blood of the Lord. Let a man examine himself" (1 Cor 11:27-28).

Ninth Bead: There is a profound analogy between Mary's "fiat" (let it be done unto me), upon which she conceives the Body and Blood of Christ, and the faithful's "Amen" (I believe) upon which we receive the Body and Blood of the Lord. Hence, fiat, Mary conceives the Body and Blood; Amen, I receive the Body and Blood (Pope John Paul II: *"Encyclical on the Most Holy Eucharist"* (55)).

Tenth Bead: The mutual consent that husband and wife exchange in Christ also has a Eucharistic dimension. Indeed, in the theology of Saint Paul, conjugal love is a sacramental sign of Christ's self-giving love for His bride, the Church, a love culminating in the Cross, which is the origin and heart of the Eucharist (Pope Benedict XVI: *Sacramentum Caritatus* (27)).

Personal Notes:

The Sorrowful Mysteries

First Sorrowful Mystery

Jesus Undergoes Temptation and Anguish in the Garden of Gethsemane

First Bead: Jesus and the apostles enter the garden where Jesus begins to experience temptation and dread. Here the abyss of sin and evil penetrate deep within His soul. Here he is betrayed and abandoned. Here He comes face-to-face with raw, naked evil.

Second Bead: His human will has some autonomy from His divine will so that He can freely choose obedience and thus atone for Adam's disobedience. The tempter attacks (Brian Mullady OP: *"Captivated by the Master"*).

Third Bead: Because He is the Son, Jesus sees with full clarity what is in the cup that He must drink to the dregs. All the sin, evil, and enmity with God for which He must make atonement.

Fourth Bead: Jesus prays: "Father if you are willing take this cup away from me; still, not my will but yours be done" (Lk 22:42). There is a natural fear of death. *Is there some other way that I can accomplish my mission?*

Fifth Bead: To obey His Father, Jesus must take on the world's disobedience; to show His love for His Father, He must take on the world's hatred. He must live this as a complete contradiction. And so in anguish He soaks the earth with His blood.

Sixth Bead: Knowing that He is facing the final decisive battle between good and evil, light and darkness, life and death, Jesus' prayer becomes one long impassioned plea for life. (Pope Benedict XVI: *Jesus of Nazareth: Holy Week,* p. 163).

Seventh Bead: Jesus seeks solace from His companions but finds them asleep. He admonishes them: "Peter could you not keep watch with me for one hour?" (Mk 14:37). The head of the Church must be especially alert.

Eighth Bead: "Watch and pray that you may not undergo the test" (Mk 14:38). The call to vigilance emerges with great urgency. Across the centuries the drowsiness of the disciples opens up possibilities for evil.

Ninth Bead: Jesus prays again: "Father if it is not possible that this cup pass without my drinking it, your will be done!" The natural will of Jesus is taken up into His personal will and He freely accepts His destiny.

Tenth Bead: Come, look, my betrayer is at hand.

Personal Notes:

Second Sorrowful Mystery

Jesus Undergoes a Roman Scourging

First Bead: Crucify Him! Pilate, not wanting to condemn an innocent man, tries to appease the crowd by ordering that Jesus should be scourged. Help me to overcome human respect and cowardice and to always do what is morally right.

Second Bead: The Roman scourge had leather thongs embedded with lead pellets and sharp pieces of bone designed to bruise and rip the prisoner's flesh into shreds.

Third Bead: Jesus' pure and holy body, so sensitive to pain, is scourged to atone for our sins of the flesh. We must mortify our passions on a daily basis and pray to God to grant moral purity to the young (Pope John XXIII: *Rosary Meditations*).

Fourth Bead: He was wounded for our transgressions (Isaiah 53:5). Out of His love for us, He accepts the agony so that we, in justice, need not experience it.

Fifth Bead: Jesus bore the indescribable pain of the scourging in heroic silence. Remember that the next time you feel like complaining.

Sixth Bead: Think of how Jesus' Mother must have felt as she watched her Son undergo this barbaric torture.

Seventh Bead: The physical devastation that scourging wreaks on the body provides an image of the effect of sin in the human soul.

Eighth Bead: Jesus finally collapses and falls to the ground. He is in great pain, bleeding heavily and half dead.

Ninth Bead: *Ecce homo*! Behold the man!

Tenth Bead: "So great was my distress when I thought how poorly I had repaid Him for those wounds that I felt as if my heart were breaking, and I threw myself down beside Him, begging Him to give me strength once for all so that I might not offend Him" (Saint Teresa of Avila).

Personal Notes:

Third Sorrowful Mystery

Jesus Is Crowned with Thorns

First Bead: The brutal soldiers clothe Jesus' badly-wounded body with an old purple cloth and then drive a crown of thorns into His head. The crown makes Him a mock king and they exclaim, "Hail, King of the Jews."

Second Bead: After Adam and Eve sinned, God cursed the ground and it yielded thorns. By accepting a crown of thorns, Jesus now takes the curse upon Himself.

Third Bead: The soldiers strike the crown with a reed, driving the thorns into Jesus' scalp. Blood from the new, very painful wounds blind His eyes. *All of this blood, Jesus, is a sign of your love for us.*

Fourth Bead: Think about who it is that is being treated this way. Out of contempt, the soldiers mock Him and strike Him on the face. Out of humility, Jesus accepts this and thus atones for our sin of pride.

Fifth Bead: Let us also bear with humility the faults of others. Let not the bride be crowned with roses while the bridegroom is crowned with thorns (Saint Charles de Foucauld). Blessed are the meek.

Sixth Bead: Anytime you think you've endured enough for Christ, remember how He was crowned with thorns.

Seventh Bead: Our own love can become, as it did for Jesus, a crown of thorns.

Eighth Bead: Let us remember all those who suffer from severe headaches.

Ninth Bead: Jesus' Passion is Mary's Compassion. *Mother of Sorrows, Queen of Martyrs, pray for us.*

Tenth Bead: His crown of thorns have won for us a crown of glory.

Personal Notes:

Fourth Sorrowful Mystery

Jesus Carries the Cross

First Bead: Pilate sentences Jesus to die. Jesus does not merely accept the cross, seeing in it the Father's will, He embraces it out of love for the Father and love for us. *Let me walk along side of You, making Your cross lighter, not heavier.*

Second Bead: On this Via Doloroso, Jesus meets His Blessed Mother. What thoughts must have gone through their minds as they looked at each other. They pierced His body, and they pierced her maternal heart.

Third Bead: Weak from loss of blood and from shock, Jesus falls under the weight of the cross. *Dear Jesus, please forgive me as it was the weight of my sins that made your cross so heavy.*

Fourth Bead: The soldiers make Simon of Cyrene carry the cross beam for Jesus. They are afraid that Jesus might die on the way to Calvary; whereas, they want to unfurl Him like a banner of warning on the cross. *When you need me, Jesus, please help me to respond.*

Fifth Bead: A woman named Veronica comes forward and, using her veil, wipes the blood from Jesus' face. Jesus leaves the image of His countenance on her cloth. Such a small act of kindness, such a great reward. *Lord, grant me a share of Veronica's courage and her love.*

Sixth Bead: Jesus meets some women who are weeping over Him. He tells them, "do not weep for me but for yourselves and your children" (Lk 23:28). Instead of thinking of Himself, Jesus shows compassion for what awaits Jerusalem in the future. Think of what will happen to you if you die in your sins.

Seventh Bead: Arriving at Calvary the soldiers strip Jesus of His garments, taking from Him the last thing He owns on earth. Soon, He will not have even a square inch of ground beneath Him. But He willingly gives all. *Lord, let me not become overly attached to the things of this earth.*

Eighth Bead: Let us also embrace with love and trust whatever suffering we must endure.

Ninth Bead: And let us pray for all others who suffer: the old, the sick, the poor, orphans, prisoners, and the persecuted.

Tenth Bead: "If any man would come after me, let him deny himself and take up his cross and follow me" (Lk 9:23). Created in the image of God, it is by losing ourselves that we find ourselves.

Personal Notes:

Fifth Sorrowful Mystery

Jesus Dies on the Cross

First Bead: The large nails crash through His wrists and ankles. "Father, forgive them for they know not what they are doing" (Lk 23:34). In His first prayer from the Cross, Jesus announces that His death will bring about reconciliation.

Second Bead: The passersby and the chief priests mock Jesus. "Let Him come down from the Cross" (Mt 27:42). If He did come down, He would have won their admiration but not their salvation. Love, not the nails, keeps Him on the Cross.

Third Bead: "Jesus, remember me when you come into your kingdom" (Lk 23:42). The freedom fighter, who, to criminalize him, has been labeled a thief, asks for mercy. "This day you will be with me in paradise" (Lk 23:43). It is never too late to turn to Jesus.

Fourth Bead: "Woman, behold your son" (Jn 19:26). The beloved disciple is given to Mary as a new son. Soon all beloved disciples will call Mary blessed Mother.

Fifth Bead: "My God, my God, why have you forsaken me?" (Mt 27:46). Praying Psalm 22, Jesus brings the world's anguished cry at God's absence before the heart of God, Himself (Pope Benedict XVI: *Jesus of Nazareth: Holy Week,* p. 214).

Sixth Bead: All of Psalm 22 is present to Jesus, including the certainty of an answer to be revealed in the Resurrection. It is a cry of hope, even in darkness, and not of despair.

Seventh Bead: Stretched out on the Cross, Jesus cries out: "I thirst!" He thirsts for our love but the soldiers offer Him vinegar. Recall the song of the vineyard. God laments that He planted a vineyard inasmuch as it yielded wild grapes. It yielded vinegar instead of wine (Pope Benedict XVI: *Jesus of Nazareth: Holy Week,* p. 218).

Eighth Bead: From noon onward the sun refuses to shine (Lk 23:44). Nature herself is too ashamed to look at the complete rejection and murder of God.

Ninth Bead: Jesus' last words are: "It is finished!" (Jn 19:30). He has completed the task His Father sent Him to do. Sin, Satan, and death are defeated.

Tenth Bead: A Roman soldier pierces Jesus' side with a lance and water and blood emerge from His sacred body (Jn 19:34). Water and blood, baptism and Eucharist, the Church, the new Eve, coming forth from the side of the new Adam. Surely, this man was the Son of God.

Personal Notes:

The Glorious Mysteries

First Glorious Mystery

Jesus Rises from the Dead

First Bead: Jesus is risen from the dead. Without this there is nothing; with this there is everything. No one else has any good news, because no one else has any news.

Second Bead: The rosary invites us to pass beyond the darkness of the Passion in order to gaze upon Christ's glory in the Resurrection.

Third Bead: "Exult, let angel ministers of God exult, let the trumpet of salvation sound aloud our mighty King's triumph!" (The Exsultet).

Fourth Bead: "Be glad, let earth be glad as glory floods her, ablaze with light from her eternal King" (The Exsultet).

Fifth Bead: "Rejoice, let Mother Church also rejoice, arrayed with the lightning of His glory" (The Exsultet).

Sixth Bead: The long reign of sin is ended, a broken world has been renewed, and man is once again made whole.

Seventh Bead: "Why are you looking for the living one among the dead?" (Lk 24:5). Jesus is now the truly living one, the eternally living one.

Eighth Bead: His love was as strong as death; His love demanded eternity (Song of Songs 8:6).

Ninth Bead: "If we have been united with Him through a death like His, we shall also be united with Him in the resurrection" (Rom 6:5).

Tenth Bead: Jesus said to Thomas, "You believe because you've seen me. Blessed are those who haven't seen and have believed" (Jn 20:29).

Personal Notes:

Second Glorious Mystery

Jesus Ascends Triumphantly into Heaven

First Bead: Jesus ascends triumphantly into heaven where He receives dominion and glory and kingship (Dan 7:14).

Second Bead: "All authority has been given to me. Go, therefore, and make disciples of all nations" (Mt 28:18-19). "You will be my witnesses in Jerusalem and to the ends of the earth" (Acts 1:8).

Third Bead: "Then He raised His hands and as He blessed them He parted from them and was taken up to heaven" (Lk 24:50-51). Jesus departs in the act of blessing and His hands are still stretched out over the world. This blessing remains in their hearts (Pope Benedict XVI: *Jesus of Nazareth: Holy Week*, pp. 292-293).

Fourth Bead: Jesus does not ascend to a different location but to a different dimension where He is close to the Father and, hence, still close to us.

Fifth Bead: Let us rejoice not only for Jesus, but also for ourselves, for if the Head is in heaven, the Church, His Body, must, in some sense, also be there. "From now on our citizenship is in heaven" (Phil 3:20).

Sixth Bead: Jesus ascends not only as Son of God, but also as Son of Man. He makes room for mankind in the love and life of the Trinity.

Seventh Bead: After the ascension, the presence of Our Lady brings consolation to the members of the early church.

Eighth Bead: The Church, the Body of Christ, must now continue Christ's work on earth. "As the Father sent me, so am I now sending you" (Jn 20:21).

Ninth Bead: Jesus' ascension corresponds to the theological virtue of hope, the hope that we too might one day follow Him into heaven to be with God the Father forever (John 14:2-3).

Tenth Bead: "And I will ask the Father and He will send you another Paraclete to be with you forever, the Spirit of Truth" (Jn 14:16).

Personal Notes:

Third Glorious Mystery

The Holy Spirit Descends Upon the Church

First Bead: We recall Pentecost, which reveals the Church gathered together with Mary and enlivened by the powerful outpouring of the Holy Spirit.

Second Bead: "When this Spirit of Truth comes, He will lead you into all truth and declare to you the things that are to come" (Jn 16:13). "He will teach you all things and call back to your mind all that I told you" (Jn 14:26).

Third Bead: The Spirit whom the Son sends is the Spirit of the eternal dialogue of love between Father and Son. This language of God becomes the Church's mother tongue. The first word we learn to speak is "Abba" (Gal 4:6).

Fourth Bead: "All that are led by the Spirit of God are children of God" (Rom 8:14). "The love of God that has been poured into our hearts by the Spirit that has been given to us" (Rom 5:5).

Fifth Bead: "Do you not know that your bodies are temples of the Holy Spirit?" (1 Cor 6:19). "No one can say that Jesus is Lord without the Holy Spirit" (1 Cor 12:3).

Sixth Bead: "You will receive power when the Holy Spirit comes upon you" (Acts 1:8).

Seventh Bead: "If you being evil know how to give your children good things, how much more will the heavenly Father give the Holy Spirit to those who ask Him?" (Lk 11:13). When God gives, He gives Himself.

Eighth Bead: When we do not know how to pray as we ought, the Spirit prays for us with sighs too deep for words (Rom 8:26).

Ninth Bead: The gifts of the Holy Spirit are wisdom, understanding, knowledge and counsel, fortitude, piety and fear of the Lord (Isaiah 11:1-3). The fruits of the Spirit are love, joy and peace, patience, kindness and generosity, meekness, fidelity and self-control (Gal 5:22).

Tenth Bead: Pentecost—the lighting of that fire that was destined to inflame the whole world.

Personal Notes:

Fourth Glorious Mystery

Mary Is Assumed Body and Soul into Heaven

First Bead: Mary is assumed body and soul into heaven. This is the final action of grace in a woman whose life was full of grace.

Second Bead: Jesus does not permit decay to touch the sinless body of His mother, the purest tabernacle of God, from which He received His precious flesh and blood.

Third Bead: "Behold, my beloved speaks to me: 'Arise, make haste, my love, my dove, my beautiful one, and come'" (Song of Songs 2:10).

Fourth Bead: The Father, Son, and Holy Spirit receive with honor their Daughter, Mother, and Spouse. So great is her majesty that the angels ask: "Who is she?"

Fifth Bead: Saint John reports seeing a vision of Mary as heaven's sun-clothed mother and twelve-starred Queen (Rev 12:1).

Sixth Bead: Many others have reported visions of Our Lady.

<u>Seventh Bead</u>: Mary's tomb in the Church of the Dormition is empty. No other tomb or reliquary makes the claim: "Here lies Mary."

<u>Eighth Bead</u>: All of Mary's other feasts are under the shadow of the Cross. The Assumption of Mary is a feast of complete joy.

<u>Ninth Bead</u>: Pope Pius XII has declared the Assumption of Mary to be a dogma of the Church.

<u>Tenth Bead</u>: The Assumption of Mary is a feast of complete joy not only for Mary, but for all of her children as it is the definitive beginning of the glory that awaits every redeemed member of the Church.

Personal Notes:

Fifth Glorious Mystery

Mary Is Crowned Queen of Heaven and of Earth

First Bead: Mary is crowned queen of heaven and of earth. This is supported by the fact that in Saint John's vision she wears a crown of twelve stars and is clothed with the sun, that is, with a glory exceeding that of all the blessed.

Second Bead: Mary is the queen mother of the King of kings. As a result, Jesus now provides for all our needs through the intercession of her Immaculate Heart.

Third Bead: Mary's salutary influence on the Church flows forth from the superabundance of the merits of Christ, rests on His mediation, and draws all of its power from it.

Fourth Bead: All the angels in heaven venerate her.

Fifth Bead: All the patriarchs and prophets in heaven venerate her.

Sixth Bead: All the apostles, martyrs, confessors, virgins, and saints in heaven venerate her.

Seventh Bead: And you and I, we venerate her.

Eighth Bead: "He has cast down the mighty from their thrones and raised up the lowly one" (Lk 1:52).

Ninth Bead: Mary persevered to the end. And now a crown is placed upon her head, a symbol of the crown of sainthood that awaits each one of us, if only we follow her example, by following her Son.

Tenth Bead: Hail, Holy Queen.

Personal Notes:

About Leonine Publishers

Leonine Publishers LLC makes fine Catholic literature available to Catholics throughout the English-speaking world. Leonine Publishers offers an innovative "hybrid" approach to book publication that helps authors as well as readers. Please visit our web site at www.leoninepublishers.com to learn more about us. Browse our online bookstore to find more solid Catholic titles to uplift, challenge, and inspire.

Our patron and namesake is Pope Leo XIII, a prudent, yet uncompromising pope during the stormy years at the close of the 19th century. Please join us as we ask his intercession for our family of readers and authors.

www.leoninepublishers.com

www.ingramcontent.com/pod-product-compliance
Lightning Source LLC
Chambersburg PA
CBHW041929040426

42445CB00018B/1949